AF413177

Aunty Kenisha Presents The Kimmy Goes Series

# Kimmy Goes To The Beach

Author: Kenisha Sprauve

Production: Stella Maze

# DEDICATION

This book is dedicated to my children, J'dya and J'bari and my niece CeRaiyah. Their younger days gave inspiration to Kimmy and her adventures.

Kimmy is excited about spending the day
at the beach.

Kimmy likes the beach because of all the treasures she will find and fun things she will see.

It is time to go to the beach. Kimmy is dressed in her pretty swimsuit. She grabs her goggles, her shovel and her bucket.

Kimmy hops in the car with her mom, dad and brother.
They are off to the beach.

The beach is Kimmy's favorite place. She likes to feel the warm
sun on her skin and the sand under her feet.

Kimmy sees a yacht. She imagines how much fun it will be to go sailing on the yacht.

Kimmy closes her eyes. She can feel the sea breeze and the
saltwater splashing on her face as she imagines
going sailing on the yacht.

Kimmy plays in the sand with her brother. They try to make sandcastles.

The sandcastles look funny, but Mom says they look beautiful.

While digging in the sand, Kimmy finds the most beautiful and shiny shell she has ever seen. She picks it up, looks closely at it and carefully puts it in her bucket.

Kimmy's brother sees something moving on the sand.

It's a crab running across the sand! They run after the crab.

It's time to go swimming. Kimmy puts on her lifejacket and
runs to the water.

Splash! Kimmy jumps in the water. The water is so clear.

Kimmy has on her googles and can see the fish swimming.

Splash! It's a pelican. It scares Kimmy. Is the pelican trying to eat Kimmy? No! It is trying to get its favorite meal, a fish.

Wow! Dad sees an orange starfish hiding in the sand.

It looks spiky. Kimmy holds it in her hands. She is not afraid of the starfish.

Kimmy wants to take it home but Mom says no. If it stays out of the water it will die. So Kimmy quickly puts it back in the water.

It's time to leave, the sun is going down.  Kimmy had
so much fun splashing and playing around.
Mom says they will be back soon.

# ABOUT THE AUHTOR

Author, Kenisha Sprauve, is an Early Childhood Education Teacher with a Master's in Education. During her many interactions with the children whom she has come in contact with, she has adapted the name Aunty Kenisha.

Aunty Kenisha enjoys helping young children reach their full potential.